Having served in the British Merchant Navy for 13 years, Roger Lancaster taught as a college lecturer, living in Bristol with his wife, Rosemary, and four children. He became a Christian at the age of 45. For more than 35 years since then, he has served as a churchwarden and undertaken many lay duties in the church. He is a speaker for the Christian charity Mercy Ships and has served time as a volunteer crew member aboard their hospital ship in West Africa.

THE OUTSIDER'S GUIDE TO CHRISTIANITY

Roger Lancaster

AUSTIN MACAULEY PUBLISHERS™

LONDON • CAMBRIDGE • NEW YORK • SHARJAH

A CIP catalogue record for this title is available from the British Library.

ISBN 9781528991476 (Paperback)
ISBN 9781528991483 (ePub e-book)

www.austinmacauley.com

First Published (2021)
Austin Macauley Publishers Ltd
25 Canada Square
Canary Wharf
London
E14 5LQ

Table of Contents

Foreword 7

The Bible 8

God 12

Jesus 17

The Holy Spirit 21

The Church 23

The Devil 27

Heaven and Hell 30

Miracles 32

Sin 34

Sex and Marriage 37

Forgiving Others 39

Bad Things Happen 40

Praise and Prayer 44

While There's Life, There's Hope 51

Foreword

Many people today know very little about Christianity unless they have been brought up in a Christian family. It is taught in many schools, most effectively when taught by those who are Christian believers themselves, but as we get older, we often remember failing to listen properly to many lessons given to us in our childhoods which we later regret. It may be talked about in pubs or other social gatherings but those giving their opinions are often not really aware of why people attend church or look to the Bible for guidance. Many people have views about what Christianity is, even strong views, without having looked into the subject properly. I was just such a person for the first 45 years of my life.

Television and other media portray priests, vicars and other Christians, but this is usually produced by non-Christians for dramatic purposes and much of it is unbelievable to Christians and gives a false impression of how the vast majority of Christians behave and what they believe.

Of course Christianity is described in great detail in the Bible, but the Bible is a large volume of 66 different books and would take a very long time to read and absorb fully, so most turn away from making the effort. This book gives a short introduction to Christianity for people who know little or nothing of the subject, to give them a better understanding of their Christian family members and friends and other Christians they meet.

The Bible

The Bible is a book accepted by Christians and others to be written by people who received the words from God through the Holy Spirit (see later) and the Bible is therefore often known as the word of God (Jesus Christ is sometimes called the Word of God, with a capital W).

The Bible is a large volume containing 66 separate books. It is in two parts. The first part, called the Old Testament (meaning old truth) has 39 books and the New Testament 27. Each book contains a number of chapters and verses and both chapters and verses are numbered.

The Old Testament tells of God's creation of the world and God's dealings with his chosen people, the Jews, or Israelites, from the beginning of the world until about 400 BC. The New Testament tells of God's later dealings with the Jews and all other peoples of the world through Jesus Christ from 1 AD onwards.

Some even larger Bibles contain a third part between the two Testaments called the Apocrypha which has 15 books. Some of these are very similar to parts of the Old Testament and it also contains other books which cover God's dealings with the Jews between 400 BC and the birth of Jesus Christ.

Orthodox Jews only accept the Old Testament and Apocrypha. While Christians accept all three parts, they are mainly **New Testament people**, but accepting the Old Testament and the Apocrypha as a true account of God's dealings with the Jews and leading on towards the coming of Jesus, the Messiah, the liberator of the Jews promised by God. Some Jews also accept the New Testament and they are called Messianic Jews because they accept that Jesus Christ is their Messiah and they are therefore Christians. Orthodox Jews believe their Messiah has not yet come. The Koran, the book of Islam, reiterates parts of both the Old and the New Testaments.

The Bible tells of three of God's "Covenants" (instructions God has given to the people of the earth and his promises to them). The first was made to Noah after the Flood and is described early in the first Old Testament book of Genesis. The second was given to Moses and can be seen in the Old Testament book of Exodus. The third was given through Jesus Christ and is covered throughout the New Testament. Jews accept the first two and Christians accept all three, but Christians believe the third, through Jesus, is more important to us, extending as it does beyond the second given to Moses.

The first book of the Bible is Genesis and covers the creation of the world by God and his dealings with the first humans, Adam and Eve, and their descendants, through the Flood, and then with Abraham and his descendants up to their time in Egypt around 1250 BC.

The second book is Exodus which covers the escape of the Israelites from slavery in Egypt and their journey into the desert. Their 40 years in the desert, during which God trains them in readiness for the land which he has promised them, is covered by Leviticus, Numbers, Deuteronomy and Joshua and leads up to their conquest of Canaan at around 1030 BC. That land became Israel from then on.

The rest of the Old Testament describes God's dealings with the Israelites from 1030 BC to 400 BC, especially about their kings and prophets, although some books are full of song lyrics, poems and words of wisdom by kings David and Solomon.

The first four books of the New Testament – Matthew, Mark, Luke and John – are called the Gospels, attributed to these four different witnesses of the birth, life, death and resurrection (bringing back to life) of Jesus Christ. Matthew and John were two of Jesus's disciples (his chosen special followers) so they were eye-witnesses to everything that happened. The fifth book, the Acts of the Apostles, tells of the experiences of the earliest Christians and the rest of the New Testament is a series of letters written by the early teachers of Christianity. The last book, Revelation, is an account of dreams and visions given by God to Saint John towards the end of his long life.

There are several versions of the Bible. The original version is written in a mixture of Greek and Hebrew. The first Bible to be written in English is the King James, or Authorised, version. More recent versions include the New International Version (NIV), the New English Bible, the Good News Bible (which uses the simplest wording) and the Living Bible (which uses very modern language). These and other editions of the Bible were all created by going back to the earliest Greek and Hebrew versions. Their wordings are different but their meanings are all the same.

Many people today regard the Bible in the same way as they think of Greek mythology and do not believe it is true. The Bible is often ridiculed yet eventually new findings will often justify it. In Genesis, chapter 3, verse 14, God punishes the snake for tempting Eve by making it crawl along on its belly, implying that it previously had legs. How ridiculous, people have said for centuries, snakes have never had legs. Yet recently scientists have found that snakes did indeed once have legs. Another example is the Pool of Bethesda, where Jesus performed a miracle of healing (John, chapter 5). The Bible says the pool had five porticos (porches) which would imply it was five-sided, yet nowhere in the Roman Empire was such a building ever heard of and it was said for many years that this proved the Bible to be untrustworthy or even made up. Yet when the building was unearthed in the late 19th century it was found to be four sided, with a portico in each side wall as expected, but there was a fifth wall dividing it into two halves and this fifth wall also had its own portico, making five in all.

Opposition to Biblical truth continues today. George and Ira Gershwin wrote a song called "It Ain't Necessarily So" which ridiculed the Bible, some comedians have made whole careers for themselves by mocking the Bible and books continue to appear which make sensational claims that the Bible cannot be trusted, and these always sell very well.

What could be described as really sensational is that the Bible is the word of God and therefore totally true. This is what Christians believe and the rest of this book may explain why that is so.

God

Christians believe in God who created the whole universe and has a special interest in our own little world. Without God there could be no Christianity.

Most of the world's religions believe there is a God. The obvious ones are Judaism, Christianity and Islam. Although Hindus have many thousands of gods, they generally believe that Brahma is the creator god and that all the others are different reincarnations of Brahma. Put all these together and you have a vast number of the world's population who believe there is a God who created the world and remains interested in it and its people. As the title implies, belief in God will be viewed from the Christian perspective in this book.

Some people worship other gods, made or pictured as animals or superhuman beings, rather like the aliens we see portrayed in science fiction films. The ancient Greeks and Romans had many such gods which are now regarded as mythology. Many more such **idols** were worshipped in most parts of the world in years gone by and some still are. Christians believe these idols were invented for various reasons and probably by the Devil. Buddhism is not so much a religion as a way of life (the Buddha was actually an Indian prince) but Buddhist temples will have images of the Buddha which appear to be very similar to those of idols.

Atheists believe there is no God. Agnostics wonder whether there is a God or not, but cannot make up their minds. Oppositions to a creator God appear more believable to many because they reject anything which we call the supernatural. But Christians in general regard the whole universe and our world, which we know exists, to be no less "supernatural" than a creator God.

Christians and other believers in a creator God are fully aware of opposing theories but have made their decisions.

As far as Christians are concerned, the Bible tells them the historic evidence for God, as experienced by Abraham, Moses, the Prophets, Jesus and his Apostles and many other lesser known characters. They believe the Bible to be true, from God, and not invented for whatever purpose. Many of these Christians have had experiences, such as miraculous healings or events which have shocked them into repentance for their sins, experiences which convince them that there is a God who even knows them personally, as the Bible tells them. Others believe because they accept the witness of people who have had these experiences. Yet others simply cannot believe that everything in the universe, including all the life on our earth – both animal and vegetable – can have appeared as a result of millions of amazing chemical accidents, and that there must be some divine designer of it all, namely the God of the Bible.

Most of these believers in God, both Christians and others, believe there is another life after death and that they will be subject to God's judgement after their death on earth as the Bible says (Romans, chapter 14, verse 10).

Christians do not see modern science regarding the beginning of the universe or evolution as in any way evidence that there is no God. They see no reason why scientists are not simply gradually discovering the ways God created everything and made life develop. Science has to be re-written regularly as new discoveries are made.

It is often claimed that the Bible says that human life is only 4,000 years old, but the Bible does not state this. This timescale is based on adding up the life times of people mentioned in Genesis, but the Bible writings are often metaphorical, especially in the Old Testament, and we do not know if the Bible gives a full list or only lists the most significant people of a much longer time. The Bible also says that a thousand years is just a day to God (Psalm 90, verse 4), implying that God's timing is not the same as ours, based as

13

ours is on the rising and setting of our sun, whereas God's might be based on something quite different.

Agnostics struggle to decide whether a creator God is true or not. They may read the Bible and books declaring the Bible to be untrue, but how can they decide which of these conflicting beliefs **is** true? This is what really matters to all of us, and we should not take our decision lightly, since what we decide will determine how we conduct our lives and how we will face death. Proof is not available to everyone's satisfaction so agnostics, if they want to make a decision, have to decide which they believe is true. There is no point in believing something which is not true. There is no point in choosing to believe something because it sounds attractive unless we are as convinced as possible that it is true. And if we are convinced something is true, but there are some things about it which make us feel uncomfortable, it is better to accept it and seek to come to terms with it than to choose something which sounds more attractive but is untrue. Some people say "what is true for you is not true for me" and vice versa, but that is to change the meaning of the words truth and falsehood. Using the long-accepted meanings of the words, whatever is true is true for everyone and whatever is false is false for everyone.

The Bible says we are made in the image of God. This cannot mean we are the same as God, but there must be something about us which is like God. Perhaps it is because we can discuss these things while animals and plants cannot. So if there is a God and we are something like him, why does he not reveal himself to us in ways we can understand and which will prove he exists? (Most Christians refer to God as male because Jesus called God his father.)

I sometimes think God has been trying to tell us he exists over many centuries, even millennia, but while we have understood some aspects, we have not usually got the whole message. The Pharaoh Akhenaten caused havoc in ancient Egypt by believing in a creator God and regarding all previous gods as false, but he decided that this god of his must be the sun. In Peru lines on the ground have been discovered in the

Nazca region which form pictures of animals, among other things, which can only be seen from the air at considerable height, suggesting that the makers believed there was someone "up there", but what else they believed is not known. There are other ancient interpretations of how the world began and stories of gods who need to be appeased by sacrifices for various reasons – where did they come from?

It would seem as if God is not willing to speak to us in ways we can easily understand. The Bible tells us he spoke to Moses from a burning bush (Exodus, chapter 3), to Saul, who later became Saint Paul, after first making him blind (Acts, chapter 9), to Samuel in the darkness of night (1 Samuel, chapter 3), to Job out of a storm (Job, chapter 38, verse 1) and to many others in dreams and visions. God spoke to the Old Testament prophets all the time but in ways which are not always specified. These prophets passed on the word of God they had received to anyone who would listen. A very early prophet, Melchizedek, the king of Salem, gave words from God to Abraham (Genesis, chapter 14, verse 18).

Most Christians today believe God speaks to them in various ways, but being sure it is God speaking is always a problem. Gideon had this difficulty in Judges, chapter 6, and decided to test it by asking God to perform a miracle by putting a fleece of wool on the ground through the night – if by morning there was dew on the wool but no dew on the ground, he would know the message was from God, which happened. Even after that Gideon wanted another similar proof, this time changing it to dew on the ground but not on the fleece. Only after the second miracle did Gideon accept that the message was from God. George Muller, the 19th century evangelist, in his famous tract "How to Ascertain the Will of God", describes five steps he would take over a long period of time before deciding whether he had got it right or not. Most Christians today would not go to such lengths but would test what they think is God's voice through prayer, by checking whether the Bible agrees with it or not and through what Muller called "providential circumstances" – things that happen which appear to justify or dismiss what they think may be God's voice.

But why should it be so difficult for us to make this decision? If there is a God who can do anything he likes, why can he not come down to earth and show us, so we can have proof of his existence and understand what he wants to tell us?

As far as Christians are concerned, God has done exactly that. The one thing above all others which proves to them that there is a creator God is the birth, life, death and resurrection of Jesus Christ.

Jesus

The first four books of the New Testament of the Bible tell us that God sent his only son into the world as a human being in the form of Jesus Christ to tell us about God's ways, to explain to us what the kingdom of God is and to deal with sin and the consequences of our own personal sins which cause such trouble in our world. These chapters are called the Gospels and were written by four separate witnesses of the life of Jesus. These four witnesses (Matthew, Mark, Luke and John) each saw Jesus from a slightly different viewpoint and together they form a history of his life in far more detail than that of any other person in the ancient world. At least two of these (Matthew and John) knew Jesus personally, went everywhere with Jesus, and were therefore eye-witnesses. They were written within 40 years after Jesus lived on earth and there would have been many other people still around at that time who had known of Jesus themselves. Today we can read the experiences of people who lived through the second and even the first of the world wars – far longer than 40 years ago – and we believe them because they were there, they were eye-witnesses like Matthew and John.

Anyone who wants to understand what Christians believe should read at least one of these Gospels – Matthew, Mark, Luke or John – it will not take long to do so and it will give a more accurate understanding than anything else.

Jesus was born to a young virgin called Mary. Jesus was not conceived in the usual way but by God in a way which only a creator God (who obviously can do anything) could do. Mary was given prior warning of this happening by a supernatural visit from the Angel Gabriel and, apart from telling her fiancé Joseph and her relative Elizabeth, it seems she kept it much to herself for many years. God spoke to Joseph in a dream to convince him that Mary's son was from God and that she had not been unfaithful to him. Other people somehow seemed to get wind of what was happening as well at the time – like the shepherds around Bethlehem and the three kings of the Magi – and the birth is told in the Gospels. This is the occasion which Christians celebrate at Christmas.

Mary and Joseph later had other children in the normal way but for many years these children did not realise that their elder brother Jesus was special.

Very little is told in the Gospels of Jesus' life until he reached 30, but a holy man called John the Baptist had been going around preaching that the long expected Jewish Messiah, who would save God's people (the Jews), would soon be coming.

John then proclaimed that Jesus was in fact the Messiah and people began to follow Jesus, but it was at a wedding in a town called Cana where Jesus really began to reveal who he was. The wine at the wedding reception was running out and Mary urged her son to do something about it, which she knew he could. Jesus was reluctant at first, saying his "time had not yet come" but Mary persuaded him to act and he turned a huge number of litres of water into wine – his first miracle (John, chapter 2, verses 1 to 12). Many miracles followed, always allowed by God, especially those of healing, and Jesus became famous, not only as a miracle healer, but even being able to raise people from death, also to calm a stormy sea (Mark, chapter 4, verses 35 to 41) and to walk on water (John, chapter 6, verses 16 to 21), proving to many that he was from God. Some of his healings were performed on the Jewish Sabbath, their holy day, and the Jewish leaders felt anger (and no doubt some envy) at the new upstart's rapid progress. They could see that Jesus really did perform miracles, but they said that these miracles came from the Devil and not from God.

Jesus' preaching showed that there was much more to his ministry than healing, however. He said that Judgement would follow our death and that all who repented of their sins and believed in him would escape Judgement and spend eternity with God in Heaven but others who did not repent would go to Hell. He told many parables (stories) to illustrate "the kingdom of God", which explained the way God wanted us to behave, showing honour and love to our fellow human beings and how to please God and have eternal life for ourselves.

Towards the end of his ministry, Jesus told his disciples (his chosen special followers) that he would be tried, convicted, punished and executed and that God would allow this to happen so that Jesus would pay the price for the sins of all those who repent of their sins and believe in his sacrifice for them, also that he would rise from the dead on the third day after his execution to show that he could conquer death and sin. The disciples did not want to believe he would be executed.

It happened, however, just as Jesus had said – he was crucified (nailed by hands and feet to a cross) and a spear thrust into his side, from which water and blood flowed for hours, until the Roman soldiers knew he was dead. It was a job they had to do very often so they certainly knew he was dead. The crucifixion of Jesus is remembered on Good Friday every year, called this not because it was a good thing to happen but because Jesus was so good to sacrifice himself to pay the price for our sins. The event is sometimes called the Passion of Jesus.

After his crucifixion, Jesus' body was laid in a tomb which was sealed with a huge stone. The tomb was watched over day and night by Jewish and Roman guards because neither wanted anyone to remove the body in order (as they thought) to falsely claim that he had risen from the dead as he had said would happen. In spite of all this protection, on the third day after the crucifixion the tomb was found to be empty apart from Jesus' burial clothes.

Jesus soon appeared alive and well, but still showing the scars of his crucifixion, to his disciples and also to many hundreds of other of his followers during the next few weeks. His rising from the dead is celebrated each year on Easter Sunday, the third day after Good Friday. He performed more miracles and explained to them what had happened and they now finally understood all he had been saying to them and they knew at last that Jesus was the son of God and the long-awaited Messiah. Jesus said that all who believe in him would live forever – have eternal life as he put it (John, chapter 3, verse 16).

A few weeks later Jesus ascended (rose up into the sky through the clouds) to Heaven, saying that he would one day come back to earth and begin a new age where the earth would become as God had originally planned in his creation, free from sin and death. This event is celebrated each year on Ascension Day.

Ever since people have speculated about when Jesus would return to earth, what Christians call the Second Coming. Many times, various groups have declared that Jesus would return on a certain day but all have obviously been incorrect. This should not be surprising because Jesus said he would return at a time when least expected (Luke, chapter 12, verse 40), so any date suggested is bound to be wrong. The only thing we can be certain about is that the time of Jesus' return is nearer now than it has ever been.

The disciples and many more of Jesus' followers began to preach the good news of Jesus' life, death and resurrection and the meaning of it all to anyone who would listen, as Jesus had commanded them to do, so that other people could also be saved from Judgement for their sins. These first Christians were often persecuted and many tortured and executed but they were not deterred since they knew that what they preached was **true**. They could have escaped such treatment if they had thought that all they had seen and heard about Jesus might not be true. These first **apostles** carried the good news given in the Gospels throughout the Middle East and well into Europe and Africa.

Before he went back to Heaven, Jesus told his Apostles that they would receive help and comfort from a person he called the Holy Spirit, but they did not understand what he was talking about.

The Holy Spirit

Acts, chapter 2, verses 1 to 21, tells us that a few weeks after Jesus left them the apostles were meeting together in a house when suddenly there was a loud noise which sounded like a strong wind blowing (but there was no strong wind). Also tongues of fire touching each person present appeared. Then they soon became able to talk in foreign languages which they had never learnt.

They remembered what Jesus had said about a new helper and comforter and realised that this must be an example of what he had been meaning. Jerusalem was a cosmopolitan city, with many people living there who normally spoke other languages. The apostles now discovered that together they could speak in all the different languages with which the people of the city were familiar. So they were able to tell everyone about Jesus, who he was and what he had done and said, and as a result many thousands of people from all nationalities believed in Jesus as the **Messiah** of Israel and the **Saviour** of all (Jews and non-Jews) who believed in him.

Speaking in different languages was not the only help the apostles received from the Holy Spirit. They became empowered to perform healings and other miracles, similar to the ones Jesus had done during his time with them (all with God's help). They were enabled to spread the good news about Jesus throughout the Middle East and beyond.

Saint Paul explains in more detail the gifts the Holy Spirit gives to believers in the Bible (1 Corinthians, chapter 12). They include gifts of wisdom, knowledge, teaching the Gospel, working miracles, healing, speaking in different languages (called "tongues") and being able to explain what is being said in tongues. Some are given several gifts, others just one.

The Holy Spirit, which used to be called the Holy Ghost, is the third aspect of God. So Father (God), Son (Jesus) and Holy Spirit together form one God. Christians call this the Trinity. The name Trinity is not mentioned in the Bible, it is simply a word used to save Christians all repeating "Father, Son and Holy Spirit" every time they want to stress that God has three forms within one. It is similar to one man called John being thought of as John the family man, John the builder or John the guitar player.

Christians today will pray for guidance from the Holy Spirit. Every Christian preacher will pray for it before preparing and again before preaching a sermon (talk) and any Christian doing God's work will pray for the appropriate gift of the Spirit before beginning the work and throughout it.

In the Bible, the book of Acts (The Acts of the Apostles) describes the spreading of the Gospel throughout the Middle East and into Europe and Africa. The name Christians was first used in Asia Minor (modern Turkey) and the whole number of Christian believers became known as the Christian Church.

The Church

Originally the Christian Church was simply the whole number of Christians in the world, living throughout the Middle East, although there were seven large, well-organised churches (groups) in the region at certain centres. The apostles, in particular Saints Peter and Paul, spread the news to areas further and further away and the Church began to grow. There was much opposition to it, especially from the orthodox Jewish authorities and people who believed in other gods, such as those in Rome, Greece and Egypt. Christians were persecuted and many killed for having their faith.

The Church was given a huge boost, however, when the Roman Emperor Constantine the First became a Christian. He made Christianity the true religion of the Roman Empire. This led to the birth of the Roman Catholic church, which grew rapidly to become the major religion in the Middle East, but it was also the beginning of the church becoming more political and more complicated than it needed to be.

A breakaway group from the Roman church, calling themselves the Orthodox Church, made their centre the city of Constantinople (modern day Istanbul) but this was later overcome by Islam and the Orthodox Church now exists in eastern Europe. Hundreds of years later some Christians felt the (Roman Catholic) church had fallen into bad ways and broke away to form the Protestant church. The Protestant church in turn broke up into many different "denominations", such as Anglican, Baptist, Methodist, Pentecostal, etc. However, all these churches are Christian in that they accept the words of Jesus Christ, as given in the New Testament.

Many of the different denominations usually make one subject from the Bible of special importance. The Baptist church, as its name implies, puts much emphasis on water baptism including full immersion, the Pentecostal church regards speaking in tongues to be an essential aim and the Roman Catholic church has its Pope as its leader and confessions are made to a priest. Other denominations claim they "interpret" the Bible in a more accurate way than the others, but again usually emphasising one part of the Bible above all others.

This splitting up of the church into so many denominations has caused much trouble in the past, especially between Roman Catholics and Protestants, in the form of wars, tensions and persecutions between peoples who should be common believers in the Gospel. Many people have claimed to be Christians over the centuries who did not love their neighbours as themselves, so they were not true Christians, and sadly there are still many like that today. **We are all sinners to some degree, so the Christian faith should not be judged by what people who call themselves Christians say or do but only by what Jesus said and did.**

Many Christians believe these divisions are the work of the Devil, who tries to destroy the church with a divide and rule strategy, influencing Christians into causing these divisions and giving them ideas which will turn them away from the really important thing – the Gospel itself – which is simply to love God, to trust in him and Jesus Christ and to love our neighbours as ourselves. In recent years there has been some progress in breaking down these barriers but they still exist. Some Christians have formed churches which are "undenominational" and they are usually called Christian Fellowships.

Most Christian groups meet in church buildings, led by priests of various titles depending on their status. Baptism using water such as that practised by John the Baptist, which Jesus received from John in the River Jordan, is normal (Mark, chapter 1, verses 4 to 11). Services include hymns, prayers and a sermon (a talk specifically related to one part of the Bible and not the minister's own personal views) by the priest. A special service of Eucharist, or Holy Communion, includes the eating of bread and the drinking of wine, which Jesus asked his disciples to do in remembrance of him (Luke, chapter 22, verses 14 to 20).

Voluntary giving of money to the church and to Christian charities for the poor is common but nothing is compulsory. No one has to give money or do any kind of work in order to gain eternal life, they only have to love God and love their neighbours as they love themselves and believe Jesus died to pay the penalty for their sins. The giving of money and the doing of Christian works does not add anything to the Salvation they receive as believers, they do these things only to show their gratitude to Jesus Christ for his sacrifice for them – they are acts of praise to God and Jesus Christ. Churches need money to exist, of course, but most church leaders simply pray to God to speak to their members to give what they can or what they feel is right. The major churches own lots of property and land but this does not mean they are wealthy, since the costs of running these churches are very substantial and preservation regulations prevent the older and larger ones from being sold and replaced by something less expensive to run and keep in good order.

Perhaps surprisingly the church tends to grow more quickly in areas where Christians are persecuted and its numbers reduce in places where its members are well off and living in peace with no persecution. Persecution takes many forms, from verbal criticism to denial of human rights and even to execution. Jesus told his followers that they would face persecution and this proves to many Christians who are being persecuted that they are doing the right thing as far as God is concerned. It does seem surprising that loving God and loving your neighbour as yourself should bring about such hatred at times.

Today's church remains largely broken up into smaller parts. Mistakes are often made and God's will is sometimes ignored, replaced by the latest fashionable trends in the hope that this will make church more popular, which it never does. But it remains God's church, all the believers in Jesus Christ with all their faults but sharing their trust in the Gospel and the promise of Jesus for their eternal life.

Most people have visited a church for weddings, baptisms or funerals, but attending a "normal" church service for the first time may be a daunting prospect for an outsider but church members will always welcome newcomers. Churches vary considerably in the detail of the ways they operate, so, although it is not necessary, if you want to visit any church service but are concerned about it, it is a good idea to first speak to a member of that church who can go with you the first time and explain how they do things there and so avoid any possible embarrassments.

The Devil

The Devil (or Satan, or Lucifer or Beelzebub) is the enemy of God.

The Bible makes it clear that Satan is real and a person, not a physical person but a spiritual one, who is not all powerful but who is crafty and works by putting thoughts into peoples' heads to make them say and do things contrary to God's will and so lose the benefits of being Christian. Even unbelievers can be aware that there is a power of evil in our world.

Satan tempted Jesus in the desert while Jesus was weak, suffering from hunger, having fasted for forty days and nights just before beginning his ministry, by suggesting that Jesus should perform miracles to show who he really was (Matthew, chapter 4, verses 1 to 11). The first was to turn stones into bread, the second was to jump off the roof of the temple to show that he would not be harmed. Jesus could have done both these things but neither would have done anyone any good or shown people the ways of God. Rather it would have seemed like a circus act, trivialising Jesus' ministry. It was tempting, however, because Satan was trying to make Jesus react to the suggestion that he was a fraud, but Jesus did not react. The third temptation was rather different. Satan took Jesus to a high mountain and showed him a vision of the whole world, saying that Jesus could have all of it if he would kneel down and worship Satan, but Jesus told Satan to go away and that all should worship God alone. Whether Satan would have had the power to fulfil his promise in this third temptation is doubtful but Satan is referred to in the Bible as being "the Prince of this world" and similar names, meaning that Satan does have some considerable power in our world but only until Jesus returns, and whatever power Satan does have until then can be counteracted by Christians with a strong faith through the power of the Holy Spirit.

Satan caused trouble for King David by tempting him to take a census of the Israelites (1 Chronicles, chapter 21, verse 1). This may not sound such a terrible thing for David to do but it made him show a lack of trust in God regarding God's protection of the Israelites. Satan's craftiness was in making the idea sound reasonable.

When Jesus sent seventy-two of his followers away to go and heal the sick with powers given by God they returned boasting that they had performed many miracles and had even been able to make demons obey them, but Jesus condemned them and blamed Satan for making them proud – and pride is a sin – it was really God who was doing these things through them (Luke, chapter 10, verses 17 to 20).

Saint Peter blamed Satan for tempting Ananias and Sapphira into defrauding the church of money (Acts, chapter 5, verses 1 to 11).

God would not heal Saint Paul's painful physical ailment. This was to prevent Satan from making Paul proud of himself and taking the credit for doing God's work (2 Corinthians, chapter 12, verses 7 to 10).

The bad thoughts we may sometimes have are put there by Satan and only the good thoughts are from God. The bad thoughts are not only the purely evil ones which cause suffering, death and destruction. Many may sound trivial to us but that is the way of Satan. Satan's aim is always to guide our thoughts away from the Gospel and so cause us to lose our Salvation and eternal life. Satan can put thoughts into our heads which make us feel inadequate, failures, unable to do God's will and so unworthy to receive the eternal life that Jesus promised us, even to lose our faith altogether. C. S. Lewis wrote an amusing book called "The Screwtape Letters" suggesting the ways in which the Devil works.

It is common today for people to regard the Devil as a mythical evil person, a figure of fun, with horns, a long-pointed tail who laughs at the evil things he does, something to dress up as at fancy dress parties. But the Bible is clear that Satan is real and is quite happy that we should regard him in these trivial ways, or that we should disbelieve in him or perhaps take a perverse interest in him and even admire him and try to imitate him.

The Bible tells us that Satan will cause trouble right up until the end of the age but that he will be defeated by the time of Jesus' return (Revelation, chapter 20, verses 1 to 3).

Heaven and Hell

The Bible tells us that Heaven is the place where God lives and where believers (or their souls) go after earthly death. Hell (or Hades) is the place of eternal suffering after their earthly death for those who have not repented of their sins and turned to Jesus.

Jesus said that Judgement would be like a shepherd separating his sheep from his goats, sheep on his right and goats on his left (Matthew, chapter 25, verse 32). The believers on the right will be allowed to enter God's kingdom of Heaven (verse 34) and the others on the left will be sent to the eternal fire of Hell 'which has been prepared for the Devil and his angels' (verse 41). Jesus also said that the majority of people would **not** find their way to Heaven (Matthew, chapter 7, verses 13 and 14).

In the Bible Heaven is portrayed as being:
Full of light and life (Revelation, chapter 22, 1 to 5)
A place of joy (John, chapter 16, verse 22)
A place of wonder (Revelation, chapter 4)
A place where God is (John, chapter 14, verses 1 to 4)
Where there is reward (Matthew, chapter 19, verses 27 to 30)
Where there is comfort (Luke, chapter 16, verse 25).

Hell is characterised by:
Darkness (2 Peter, chapter 2, verse 17; Jude, verse 6)
Fire (Matthew, chapter 5, verse 22 and chapter 25, verse 41).

It is difficult to imagine where these places are and what they are like and perhaps we all have different ideas about them. The Bible's descriptions seem beyond our imaginations. All we can be sure about is that Heaven is obviously good for us, while Hell is certainly bad – to be avoided at all costs – and Christians are convinced that God, who created everything, can therefore do anything, and that **Jesus always told the truth.**

Miracles

The Bible tells us in the New Testament that Jesus performed miracles, so also did his Apostles, although in all cases these could only happen through God's help.

Miracles also happened in the Old Testament. Aaron's stick was turned into a snake (Exodus, chapter 7, verse 10), the Red Sea parted to allow the Israelites through but not the Egyptians (Exodus, chapter 14), Daniel's friends remained unharmed inside a blazing furnace (Daniel, chapter 3, verses 19 to 28) and there are many more.

But there were times when miracles, messages and visions from God seemed to be very rare (1 Samuel, chapter 3, verses 1 to 10).

Is that true today? Do miracles happen at all in our time? *I* know they do but the trouble with miracles is that they are usually only truly believed to be miraculous by those who witness them directly and others are often sceptical.

I have personally witnessed three amazing miracles in my (more than) 80 years and many other happenings which were most likely miracles. One of the three took place only two years before I write this.

I have told people of these three miracles a few times but although they are polite, I sense their scepticism. I feel that they are thinking things like "it's just incredible good luck" or "there must be some logical reason for it". You can always say these things where miracles are concerned – the only "logical" reason is that they are performed by God. Unbelievers will make these comments even if they have witnessed a miracle themselves. I know that these three happenings were miracles but two of them were personal, for me alone. The most recent one involved me going through a frightening experience from which I escaped in a way that I could only explain as miraculous and I believe God was giving me a lesson in trust, effectively saying "Trust me, I know what I'm doing". Many Christians have experienced similar miracles.

When accidents happen people often say "it was a miracle no one was killed". It probably was, but not many people will accept this common response as being literally true. Miracles are not usually accepted as proof that there is a God.

Saint Paul knew the limits of miracles when he complained that 'Jews want miracles for proof and Greeks look for wisdom' (1 Corinthians, chapter 1, verse 22).

Jesus performed so many miracles before so many thousands of people that it was almost impossible for those around to disbelieve they were miracles and he became well known as a miracle worker and many believed it proved that he was the long-awaited Messiah. But others would have been sceptical even after seeing them with their own eyes and the Jewish leaders even said they must have come from the Devil because Jesus performed some of them on the Sabbath.

I believe that the reason why people generally do not accept events to be miracles is that miracles involve the supernatural, which is a bit spooky and hard to believe. But the foundation of the whole universe is a supernatural happening (a miracle), especially that of our own planet with its proliferation of animal and vegetable life. The whole of life is miraculous.

Sin

Sin can be described as doing, saying or thinking anything which opposes God's creation, his Son (Jesus), his Holy Spirit or his word (the Bible). Also, that if we commit sin without repenting and accepting Jesus as our Saviour, we will have to pay for it on Judgement Day after we die and be sent to Hell.

God gave us through Moses the Ten Commandments (Exodus, chapter 20, verses 3 to 17). They are:

1. Do not worship other gods.
2. Do not worship man-made objects.
3. Do not misuse God's name.
4. Keep holy the Sabbath day (Sunday) and do no work on it.
5. Honour your father and your mother, that your days may be long.
6. Do not murder.
7. Do not commit adultery (sexual conduct outside of marriage).
8. Do not steal.
9. Do not tell lies against others.
10. Do not desire other peoples' possessions.

These commandments form the basis of the Jewish law. They are there for our own good. They also form the basis of our own laws, although they have always seemed to be far too simple for man to adopt as they stand, and our modern laws are so complex that even professional lawyers have to look them up in the many books in which they are stored.

We have all broken some of the commandments – perhaps not murder or adultery or stealing – but who can claim never to have envied someone else's belongings or lifestyle, or never to have done work on a Sunday? They are all sins and the Bible does not say that some are more or less sinful than others. The Bible tells us that we are all sinners (1 John, chapter 1, verse 8). John writes, 'If we say we have no sin we deceive ourselves and the truth is not in us.'

In the New Testament Jesus condensed the commandments into just two. When he was asked about the law, Jesus said (Matthew, chapter 22, verses 37 to 40), 'Love the Lord your God with all your heart and with all your soul and with all your mind and with all your strength. This is the first and greatest commandment. And the second is like it: Love your neighbour as you love yourself. All the Law and the Prophets hang on these two commandments.' But these do not make it any easier for us. Jesus said that even a person who commits the sin of calling someone a fool will be in danger of being sent to the fire of hell (Matthew, chapter 5, verse 22).

Regarding the first of Jesus' commandments, how can we love God who we have never seen? In the first letter of John (1 John, chapter 5, verse 3) he says, 'This is love for God: to obey his commands, and his commands are not burdensome.'

The breaking of Jesus' second law (love your neighbour) by people who claimed to be Christians has given the Christian faith a bad name over the centuries: the crusaders, the Spanish inquisitors, the conquistadores, warring Roman Catholics and Protestants – all broke this law, dishonouring Christ and the faith they profess. The only person the Christian faith should be judged by is the example of Jesus Christ himself. The rest of us are sinners, as we can see if we look at the commandments.

Causing others to sin is even worse than sinning ourselves. Jesus said (Luke, chapter 17, verses 1 to 3), 'Things that cause people to sin are bound to come. But woe to that person through whom they come. It would be better for them to be thrown into the sea with a millstone round their neck than for them to cause one of these little ones to sin. So watch yourselves. If your brother sins, rebuke him, and if he repents, forgive him.'

Sex and Marriage

The general opinions of what is or is not acceptable regarding sex and marriage are numerous and can vary as times change and from country to country. Our individual opinions are often motivated by our own personal preferences at any given time. What follows in this section is **what God tells us throughout the Bible** regarding sex and marriage.

In Genesis (chapter 2), God made a man (Adam) and later a woman (Eve) so that they could help and comfort each other throughout their lives. Verse 24 says, 'For this reason a man will leave his father and mother and be united with his wife and they will become one flesh.' This single commitment for life is what the Bible calls marriage.

Marriage is not essential for Christians; indeed, the Bible says that staying single can be preferable. Advantages and disadvantages of marrying or remaining single are discussed by Saint Paul in detail in 1 Corinthians, chapter 7.

The Bible does not specify any particular kind of marriage ritual, only that a man and a woman become united. They become "one flesh", that is they behave as if they were one person and remain together until one of them dies. Their children's DNA will show it comes from both parents. This is God's will for mankind in his creation and his reason for giving us sexual activity. Any other kind of sexual activity is contrary to God's will and is therefore sin, and the Bible calls it adultery. (The earliest English Bible, the King James version, uses the word "fornication" while most modern versions use the words "sexual immorality".) Sex before and outside of marriage and sexual activity which is not between a married couple of a man and a woman is therefore adultery. The seventh commandment (Exodus, chapter 20, verse 14) says, 'You shall not commit adultery.' Even cross-dressing is adultery (Deuteronomy, chapter 22, verse 5), also even thinking of committing adultery is adultery itself (Matthew, chapter 5, verse 28).

Other unlawful sexual relationships are defined in Leviticus (chapter 18), Deuteronomy (chapter 22) and 1 Corinthians (chapter 6, verses 9 to 11).

Until fairly recently adultery was illegal in many countries but in these times many adulterous activities may no longer be illegal, but they will still be sinful in God's eyes. In these so-called enlightened days, I guess most of us have committed adultery at some time and in some form or another, even if only in thought. So any sin of adultery we have committed is yet another of the many reasons we need **Salvation**, a **Saviour**, who will pay the price for our sin and thus free us from judgement. This is why the Gospels are called good news. We will need to repent, come to Jesus and trust in him, but repentance for any sin must be sincere – God will know whether it is or not.

Many couples unite together as described in Genesis without making any formal commitments but since the Bible does not give any procedures other than "uniting" I believe they are married in God's eyes. Like people who marry conventionally, of course, they will sin if they commit adultery.

Re-marrying after the death of a spouse is not adultery (Romans, chapter 7, verses 2 and 3). Re-marrying after a divorce is adultery (Mark, chapter 10, verse 11) unless the person re-marrying is the innocent party in a divorce caused by marital unfaithfulness (Matthew, chapter 5, verse 32).

Paul gives rules for husbands, wives and children in Colossians, chapter 3, verses 18 to 21.

Forgiving Others

Even Christians can find forgiving others difficult but in Luke, chapter 17, verses 3 and 4, Jesus says, 'If your brother sins, rebuke him, and if he repents, forgive him. If he sins against you seven times in a day, and seven times comes back to you and says 'I repent,' forgive him.

In several other parts of the New Testament Jesus tells us to forgive others without mentioning that the sinner should repent first but I would suggest that the need for repentance is taken for granted. God will not forgive us if we do not repent and turn to Jesus (Psalm 66, verse 18), so I do not think he would expect us to do anything different. However, Jesus forgave those who crucified him, so forgiving others who are not sorry for what they have done would be seen by God as especially gracious, but it is not our forgiveness that they need most, it is God's. Our forgiveness alone may not help them when they come to judgement but God would like us to forgive them anyway.

Failing to forgive others makes us bitter and we want justice or revenge, but this is bad for us and it may make us unhealthy or miserable for the rest of our lives. In Deuteronomy, chapter 32, verse 35, God says 'It is mine to avenge, I will repay.' So we should leave justice and revenge to God rather than rely on our own attempts, which are themselves sins, or put too much trust in our government's flawed ways of administering justice. Forgiving regardless will please God and will give us more peace.

Christians have a special reason for forgiving others. They know that they themselves have been forgiven their sins by God because they have repented, accepted that Jesus paid the penalty for their sins and put their trust in Jesus' word.

Bad Things Happen

Atheists will say that if there is a God of love, he would not allow bad things to happen, yet we know that bad things do happen therefore there can be no God.

How can Christians deny this apparently sound logic?

The Bible says God is a God of love **and a God of wrath** (anger) (Isaiah, chapter 13) and that most of the bad things in the world come from sin (doing, saying and thinking things which God did not intend in his creation of the world).

God's wrath is shown many times in the Old Testament. God brings calamities to the Israelites in order to show them that, although he exists for them and will help them in all things as long as they obey him, if they disobey him they will suffer severely, but they never seem to get the intended message for very long. God also uses the Israelites to deliver his wrath to the enemies of Israel, all of whom worshipped idols and did very evil things – some carried out human sacrifices, even killing their own children, to appease their gods.

In the New Testament, however, God's new and third covenant, which Christians live by, there is little of God's wrath and much more of God's love for the world and its people, even those who disobey him. God's wrath remains, however, in that God cannot forgive any sinner who does not repent and turn to Jesus.

But bad things happen these days, as we all know, so if there is a loving God why does he allow such things to happen? There are times when we all think that if we were God, we would do things differently, but our knowledge is very limited and we can never see the bigger picture. In the Bible, when Job, who was a Godly person but who suffered terribly, questions God about his ways, God explains this in great detail (Job chapters 40 and 41).

Many of the bad things that happen in our world are caused by people, either through their deliberate actions or through their not realising that the things they do will cause other people harm.

So why does God not stop them from doing these things?

God does not physically stop people from doing bad or stupid things but he can send strong warnings as he did to the Pharaoh of Egypt in the form of plagues (Exodus, chapters 7 to 12) and when he gave the power of speech to Balaam's ass (Numbers, chapter 22, verses 21 to 35). If he were to physically stop people doing bad or stupid things, how would he do it? Would he strike them dead before they could act? If so, where would God draw the line? God says it is bad for us to desire things belonging to other people and to do work on a Sunday. Would we think it fair for him to strike us dead if we were about to do these things? The words we say can often damage others. How often have we said things which hurt other people? We often regret it afterwards (but it cannot be unsaid) and how would we feel if God struck us dumb before we could even say such things? It is easy to think that God should stop others from doing bad things but when it comes to ourselves, we might take a different view.

The Bible makes it clear that God wants to save sinners, to turn them around. Jesus said he did not come into the world for the righteous but for sinners (Matthew, chapter 9, verses 12 and 13). The Bible also says we are all sinners of one sort or another and will face judgement for our sins after death unless we confess them, turn around and accept that Jesus paid the price for our sins when he died on the cross (1 John, chapter 1, verse 8).

So God gives everyone every chance to turn away from their sins during their lifetime before they have to face judgement, even if this means that others suffer. When Pharaoh persecuted the Israelites in Egypt and would not let them go God did not strike him dead but he did send ten plagues to Egypt to show Pharaoh his anger and give him every chance to relent, which Pharaoh finally did (although he was not very pleased about it) and both the Israelites and the Egyptian people suffered severely for a while until then. In more recent times we have had very evil people causing wars and suffering – Hitler, Stalin, Pol Pot, Idi Amin, and so on and on. They seemed to be able to carry on for so many years before their final fall, during which time many people suffered and died as a result. If we had been in control, we would no doubt have stopped them in their tracks before much time had passed, but giving them ample time to repent would certainly fit in with God's willingness to give everyone every chance to turn away from their sins even though so many people suffer. Evil people like drug and people traffickers seem to carry on with little hindrance, causing suffering to many, but one day they will face a terrible Judgement if they do not repent and make amends where possible.

God's ways are different to ours. We might think that if we were God, we would strike these very evil ones dead before they could do any damage to those we would call innocent people, but we usually think only of this short life of ours on earth while God knows that our life in eternity is much more important, whether in heaven or hell, if only because it lasts infinitely longer.

People are killed in earthquakes, which are natural occurrences and cannot be blamed on anyone. But it is not usually the earthquake which does the killing, it is the man made buildings which collapse and the man-made vehicles which crash. If we were still all living in tents and just walking around very few people would die due to earthquakes. Everyone knows that earthquakes will happen, especially in some areas, but people still want to live there for various reasons and they hope nothing serious will happen in their lifetime. When the earthquake does one day strike, they should not blame God.

Could God stop earthquakes and floods from happening? I'm sure he could and we do not know why they need to happen, but they are part of God's creation and he will have his reasons. We know they have always happened so we should accept them and take what precautions we can to limit the effects on us. Again, we think only of our short life on earth and not on the more important eternity which follows.

Then there is sickness of many kinds which can cause us severe pain and death. If we knew what in God's creation caused these things and what we need to do to prevent them we could stop them happening, but there is so much we do not yet know about God's creation and these things will continue to happen until we do discover more.

In the book of Deuteronomy, God gives lots of instructions to the Israelites about what things are bad to eat, how to find the safest drinking water, how to deal with mildew and many more things which protect our health. At the time the Israelites did not know why they should obey these weird sounding laws but those who did take notice were kept well and those who did not became ill. We know now the scientific reasons for most of these safety laws whereas the Israelites in those days did not, but those who had faith that what God said was for their benefit remained healthy.

Praise and Prayer

Christians love God and praise his name for all sorts of reasons but chiefly because he sent his son Jesus Christ to be with us here on earth for a while, to take the penalty for our sins by dying on the cross, then rising from the dead and returning to be with his Father in Heaven.

Why should God, who created everything and is Lord of the universe, need to receive our praise? We all like to be praised, or at least appreciated for what we do or say, even though we might never admit it, so, since the Bible says we are made in the image of God, if we like these things then it is logical to think that God would appreciate them from the people he created.

In wartime it is not uncommon for people to give their own lives so that others might live (although they would not sacrifice their own children to do so). In such cases, people give their lives because they feel the ones they save deserve it. Those saved would never forget such a sacrifice given for them and would forever praise the one who saved them – their **saviour**.

But Jesus gave his life for sinners, for people like us who do not deserve it, and he did this because his Father God wanted him to. Why? Because God loves all the people he has created and wants them to live forever with him in Heaven, but he is also a god of justice and cannot allow unrepentant sinners to go unpunished (love and wrath). Since we are all sinners, no one deserves to avoid punishment. God's plan to overcome this was to send his only son Jesus into the world to pay the penalty for all those undeserving sinners who recognise that Jesus is their Saviour and frees them into eternal life. Being saved like this is called **salvation** in the

Bible, and Jesus is our **Saviour**. This was God's new (third) covenant for the people of earth.

Charles Wesley's wonderful hymn "Love divine, all loves excelling" is often used at weddings. Some people believe it is about love in general and therefore appropriate for people getting married. But it is really about the love of God who made the sacrifice of love described above, as people will realise when reading the words carefully for the first time. It is true praise for our Saviour.

So all Christians praise God, not only in church services but throughout each and every day.

Some people are better at speaking out words of praise than others. Many Christians, myself included, find praise rather difficult, our words seeming so inadequate. We therefore show our praise mostly through the words of the many thousands of hymns of praise like "Love Divine", written by people who have been given their gifts of poetry and music from the Holy Spirit.

We also praise God for the wonders of his creation, for all the good things we receive from animal and vegetable life and for the minerals we can use to make our lives better, but not least we praise God for answers to our prayers.

Jesus said (John, chapter 14, verse 14), 'You may ask me for anything............... and I will do it.'

Well, we all know that doesn't always work, don't we? The missing words in that quote are "in my name". Does this mean that all we have to do to get the answer to our prayer that we want is to include the name of Jesus in it? Anyone who has tried to pray like this will know that doesn't "work" either.

So what does Jesus mean when he says "in my name"? Christians who have prayed many times and received answers to their prayers realise that praying in Jesus' name is praying a prayer of which Jesus would approve, so the more we know about Jesus the better will be our prayers. Also, they will know from experience that there are three possible answers to a prayer: "yes", "no" or "not yet".

Jesus told a parable (Luke, chapter 18, verses 1 to 8) about a widow who kept pestering a judge to give her the justice she thought she deserved. In the end the judge gave in to the widow in case she wore him out. Does this mean that we have to keep pestering God to get what we want? A parable is just a story, so this did not really happen, but Jesus used parables to astonish people and so raise their interest in what he was saying and in this one he was trying to tell them about the "not yet" answer and to keep on praying if we are sure we are doing so according to God's will. The answer could still be "no" or it could be "not yet", in which case we should keep on praying and be patient. George Muller once said he had been praying for one person for sixty years and still had no positive answer but he kept on praying anyway because he believed that what he was asking for was according to God's will. In the Lord's prayer, given to us by Jesus himself, we pray "thy kingdom come, thy will be done, on earth as it is in Heaven" and even that prayer has not been answered yet, but we know that one day it will be answered positively because the Bible tells us so and therefore we keep on praying for it to happen, and the sooner the better.

I have received many "no" answers to my prayers. In one example, I thought I needed to change my job, so I applied for a very different kind of job and prayed that I would succeed. But my application was rejected and I was very upset and wondered why God had not answered my prayer in the way I had hoped. Shortly afterwards, however, I received a very large increase in salary in my current job, I found a new contentment in the work I had been doing for many years and the kind of job I had prayed for became obsolete soon afterwards because of changes in supply and demand. Then I was really glad God had given me the "no" answer.

Happily, I have received very many "yes" answers to my prayers which far outweigh the "no" and "not yet" answers. In particular my prayers for other people get many more "yes" answers than my prayers for myself. I do not believe that is a coincidence.

One of the hardest "no" answers to accept is the one when we pray for healing for a family member or friend and they die without having been healed. Why on earth should God not give a "yes" answer to such a prayer, especially for a young person or a Christian or one who has been a good person? All I can say is that God's creation includes the fact that we shall wither and die, at least during our time on earth, and nothing is going to change that, but it does not mean that we should not continue to pray for our sick friends and relatives – for all we know we are receiving a "not yet" answer. God may have his reasons for giving "not yet" answers – read the book of Job. If it is a "no" answer Christians know that they can trust Jesus when he says that all who believe in him will have eternal life after their death in this world and that they will then be free from all suffering.

I have sometimes wondered about Lazarus, who Jesus raised from the dead (John, chapter 11, verses 1 – 44). Jesus had seemed strangely reluctant to go to Lazarus but did so after pleading from Lazarus' sisters. But what did Lazarus think about being raised from the dead? The Bible does not tell us, but I cannot help feeling that he had died, gone to Heaven and had no more pain or suffering. Now he was dragged back to earth, back to his arthritis or whatever he suffered from. Perhaps I'm wrong in this case, but I think we should always be careful about what we wish and pray for.

Many Christians include the words "if it is your will" in their prayers. Others say that this shows a lack of faith and we are producing a get-out clause in case we do not receive the answer to prayer that we would like. However, when I remember, I always include it in my prayers because Jesus said it when he prayed to God that, if it was possible, he would not need to be crucified (Matthew, chapter 26, verse 39 and again in verse 42). It is so easy to pray for something which is not according to God's will when we don't realise it at the time.

When it comes to praying for our own healing, we will not be able to distinguish between whether we are receiving a "not yet" or a "no" answer and then we must trust God, pray for his guidance on how to deal with it and be patient. One day it will be a "no" answer, of course, but we will still not know which it is until it happens, by which time, if we have confessed all our sins and put our trust in Jesus our Saviour, we can be sure that eternal life will follow.

Most of our church services are taken up with praise and prayers. We praise God through our hymns, prayers of thankfulness and readings from the Bible, especially the Psalms. We pray for forgiveness for our own sins, for people we know who are in some kind of need, for the problems people are suffering from around the world, for God's Holy Spirit to help us in our daily lives, for the church and all that goes on in it and for many other things as well.

Two special prayers are used in almost every Christian service. They are the **Lord's Prayer**, given by Jesus to his disciples as an example of how we should pray to God (Matthew, chapter 6, verses 9 to 13) and the **Nicene Creed**, a prayer in which the people declare what they believe. There can also be a **collect**, which is a special prayer for a specific day in the Christian calendar.

The exact wording of the Lord's Prayer can vary. Church versions have been brought up to date in language, but the meaning never varies. The version used in the Church of England mostly is as follows:

> **Our Father in Heaven,**
> **hallowed be your name,**
> **your kingdom come,**
> **your will be done**
> **on earth as in Heaven.**
> **Give us today our daily bread.**
> **Forgive us our sins**
> **as we forgive those who sin against us.**
> **Lead us not into temptation**
> **but deliver us from evil.**
> **For the kingdom, the power and the glory are**
> **yours, now and forever. Amen.**

The word Amen is usually used at the end of each prayer. It is a word of confirmation of what has been said in the prayer. It is like saying "I really mean what was said in that prayer".

The wording of the Nicene Creed, or the Apostles Creed, can also vary very slightly, but again the meaning remains the same:

We believe in one God,

The Father, the almighty, maker of heaven and earth,

of all that is, seen and unseen.

We believe in one Lord, Jesus Christ, the only Son of God, eternally begotten of the Father,

God from God, Light from Light, true God from true God, begotten, not made, of one being with the Father.

Through him all things were made.

For us men and for our salvation he came down from heaven; by the power of the Holy Spirit he became incarnate of the Virgin Mary and was made man.

For our sake he was crucified under Pontius Pilate; he suffered death and was buried.

On the third day he rose again in accordance with the Scriptures; he ascended into heaven and is seated at the right hand of the Father.

He will come again in glory to judge the living and the dead and his kingdom will have no end.

We believe in the Holy Spirit, the Lord, the giver of life, who proceeds from the Father and the Son. With the Father and the Son, he is worshipped and glorified.

He has spoken through the Prophets.

We believe in one holy catholic and apostolic Church.

We acknowledge one baptism for the forgiveness of sins.

We look for the resurrection of the dead, and the life of the world to come. Amen.

While There's Life,
There's Hope

Many people who, after a long time, feel the need for salvation because of their sins believe it is too late, they have sinned too much and God will never forgive them. Christians will say that it is the Devil who brings such thoughts into their minds.

I became a Christian at the age of 45, confessed my many sins to God, turned to Jesus as my Saviour and trusted him to forgive my sins and grant me eternal life in spite of myself. If I had died at the age of 44, it would have been too late.

Jesus tells a parable of the workers in a vineyard (Matthew, chapter 20, verses 1 to 16). The farmer began hiring workers at a fixed daily rate early in the morning. Later he hired more workers at the same rate. All day he hired more workers, all at the same rate. Even at the eleventh hour (presumably a 12-hour day) the workers hired earned the same amount of money even though they had worked for just one hour. This obviously seemed grossly unfair to the people who had worked all day for the same money as those who had worked for only an hour.

But like all of Jesus' parables, it was just a sensational story to shock people into understanding that God's ways are not our ways and that those who join the Kingdom of God near the end of their lives (the "eleventh hour") receive the same benefits of life after earthly death as those who join in early childhood. (The advantage to those who join early is that they enjoy knowing God and Jesus and the promise of salvation for a longer time and so live in peace for longer.) We are all allowed our whole lives to repent and turn to Jesus but one day it will be too late and we never know when that will be.

I hope and pray that readers of this little book will now know more about what Christians believe and why, and that this will bring more understanding.

May God bless and guide you through your life on earth.